DRIFTING BETWEEN WORLDS

Paris Delaney

ISBN: 978-1-967109-18-0

Publishing Company: Author Book Publications

i

For Lana,

Everything I do, I do it for you.

"The life of the dead is placed on the memories of the living. The love you gave in life keeps people alive beyond their time. Anyone who was given love will always live on in another's heart."

— Marcus Tullius Cicero

Table of Contents

About The Author

Paris Delaney writes poetry that pulses with emotion, blending vivid imagery and raw honesty to explore the fragile, beautiful connections that define us. Her work invites readers to drift between dreams and reality, where love, loss, and self-discovery intertwine.

Paris creates poetry that resonates with anyone who has ever loved deeply or longed for something just out of reach. She lives by the sea with her husband, Sam, and their dog, Loki, drawing inspiration from the wild beauty of nature and the quiet moments in between.

A Place to Drift

Heavy mind, weary eyes,
Treading old gold trails, where truth lies.
Seeking light but finding shade,
Answers hidden, hopes betrayed.

Regressing, regressing, the cycle's snare,
Revolting, revolting, against despair.
Regretting, regretting, each step retraced,
Caught in a loop, a haunting chase.

Craving a quiet corner, an empty bed,
To lay my bones, to rest my head.
The rabbit hole beckons, a siren's call,
A velvet descent where shadows fall.

Dreams ferment, shadows loom,
A lullaby of endless gloom.
Let me drift where silence reigns,
Where echoes linger, free from chains.

In a fragile realm, half light, half gray,
Take me there, and let me stay.

Wildflowers

I awoke to a symphony of colour and scent,
In a meadow where wildflowers bow and bend.
I creaked my eyes open, sunlight poured in,
Washing over me like summer's rain.

Above me, the sky unfurled its vast expanse,
Splashed with hues- tequila sunrise dance.
Cotton candy clouds drifted by,
Framing the love painted behind amber eyes.

Tall gates stood beyond my gaze,
A whisper lingered, soft as a hymn: "Wait."
Daisies towered, their petals brushed my skin,
Not to frighten, but to pull me within.

Wildflowers swayed in the breeze,
Autumn leaves skating on whispered pleas.
The earth hummed gently, urging me near,
But as I rose, the ground disappeared.

I fell into the hollow— a hollowed burrow deep,
The meadow's whispers echoing in my sleep.

Time Dissolves

A reel rewinds,
Playing a black-and-white film.
Kindred souls smile,
Their laughter now haunting the tide.

Ghosts spill through fractured light,
Unaware of time's endless flight.
The sky splits like paper; the sea bleeds
twilight,
Waves carrying red, but never returning it.

Salt and iron linger in the air,
Vanilla clouds layer like spun silk.
Through the haze, a white rabbit darts,
Its fur a fleeting smear of motion and art.

Time unfurls—a serpent uncoiled,
Ticking steady, unrelenting.
Footfalls echo, spiraling into eternity,
Shadows flicker, dim in the waning light.

Memory dissolves as mist engulfs the minutes,
Figures blur into enigmatic silhouettes.

The Dock

Withered planks stretch to a blurred horizon,
My gaze locks on a clock, relentless—Tick, tock,
tick, tock,
Its pulse grows louder, faster, heavier.

I step closer, reaching for its face,
But the closer I get, the further it flees.
It spins and tumbles, rolling down the dock,
Diving into the waves—disappearing beneath.

The clock becomes a fractured barge,
Numbers dissolving into foam.
Its call is silent, yet I feel it—
A tremor beneath my skin, an unseen pull.

I step aboard, trembling legs unsteady,
No life jacket, no map, just endless tides.
The barge rocks hypnotically, swaying like a
pendulum,
My reflection ripples below—a fractured mirror.

I fall into the water's embrace,
Time shattering above the surface.
Here, I am nowhere—neither here nor there,
Just a hollow ache, echoing within.

A figure appears, roped and grey,
Standing at the bow, silent and still.

Without a word, he steers us deeper,
Into the mist, where hours fade to dust.

No anchor holds me, no rope binds me,
Only the pull of the unknown.
Dreams and fragile hopes guide my way,
As I search for what's been lost—over and over,
Until I am whole.

Between Worlds

I drift between the living and the dead,
Along the desolate Styx riverbed.
The air hums with eerie indifference,
Broken only by whispers overhead.

Aboard a worn barge, I roam dark passageways,
Fog lingers, thick and grey.
Like smoke, it clings to every bend,
Each curve concealing what lies ahead.

Whispers echo— guides or distractions?
I cannot tell, yet I follow blindly.
The current pulls me deeper still,
Into a world between worlds, silent and unknown.

Splinters bite my hands as I cling to the boat,
Eyes wide, searching the shadows.
No rest comes, only the ache of longing,
As the river carries me where it will.

The living world fades into the fog,
A distant memory, faint and pale.
I hold to fragile hopes, splintered truths,
Letting the current decide my fate, wherever it
may flow.

Spring Morning

From the earth, a crisp spring morning breaks—
Black tūī birds whistle atop golden kōwhai
trees.
Seagulls cry in long, winding chorus,
Gliding over skies painted with dawn.

Daffodils rise, the sun lingers warm,
The air, rich with the promise of tomorrow.
Yet I remain untouched by time—
No clocks tick here, no moments pass.

A hush of pale light spreads thin,
The air withheld, brittle and sharp.
The living world stirs— children laugh, voices
ring,
Heads bowed, people work and dream.

But I am a shadow pressed against the glass,
A figure caught in timeless reflection.
Home lies just out of reach,
Yet I travel this passage instead.

Tulips

Through a soft haze of morning fog,
I watch slender green stems rise—
Dancing in quiet harmony,
Rooted, yet swaying with quiet pride.

Purple blooms brush against the breeze,
Their voices hushed, yet certain.
Humble, mysterious— Sophia Loren at dusk,
Verdant arms drift, fingertips grazing the wind.

In a breeze-tinged reverie, they whirl,
Bowing in silent applause.
Tchaikovsky hums a floral ballet,
Each bloom— enigmatic, eternal.

A promise that beauty endures,
A living glow pressed against the hush of night,
Calling me to linger,
Just for a moment longer.

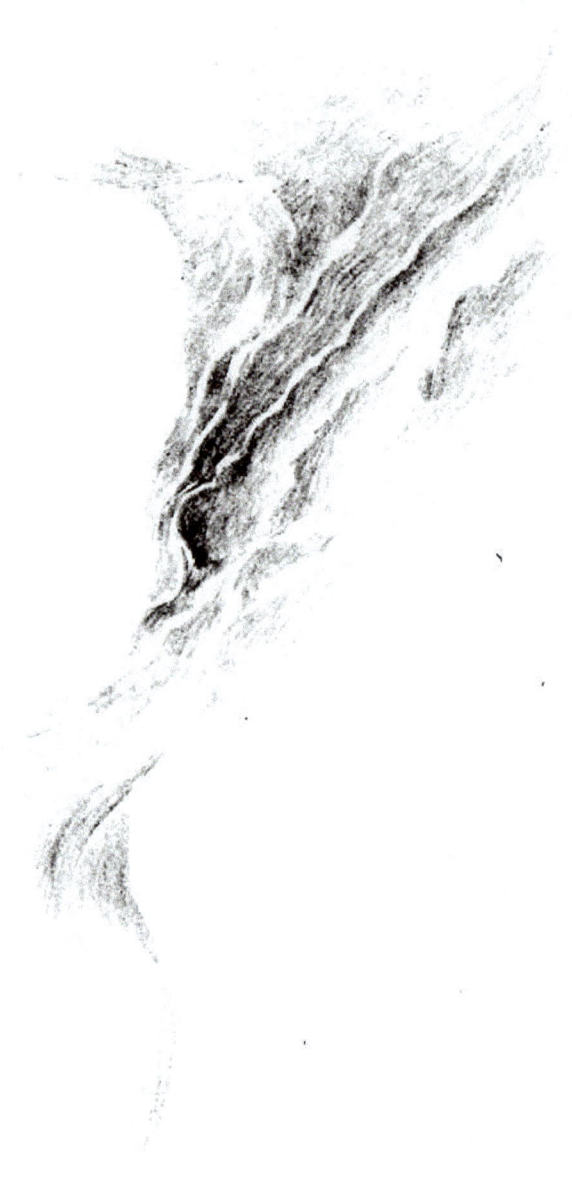

16

The Calm Before the Rain

A hushed sky whispers its warning low,
Clouds bruise violet, thick with sorrow.
The air hums sharp, humidity clings,
The scent of rain hangs, waiting to sing.

The earth holds still, bracing for change,
Roots pulse beneath the dampening soil.
The wind carries salt and copper's bite,
Leaves shiver, restless, in muted light.

The pressure builds— a pale ache blooms,
Electric, searing through my lungs.
The earth holds its breath, tight with pain,
This is the calm before the rain.

Rememberings

The sky fractures—
Not with thunder, but with a tremor.
The air bruised, heavy, waiting to break—
And then—her.

A figure behind the mist,
Fragile as light pressed through frost.
Her outline drifts—
And I remember.

It strikes—
A pulse beneath my skin,
Sharp as ice,
Blooming along my ribs.

Waves rise—
Grief spills through me,
Steady, relentless, loud,
Like the ache of something long withheld.

I see her—
Woven into the fog's pale hush,
Her face a blur, lips parted,
Calling, waiting.

I reach—
The mist cold against my palms,
Parting— just for a breath—

Before she dissolves again.

I remember now—
She was the light beneath it all.
The warmth, the pulse, the flame—
And I have been searching for her all along.

Agony

A shift in the air,
A break in the beat.
A rhythm unraveled,
A fractured melody.

Something is undone,
Not as it should be.
A faint alarm whispers,
A silent scream, unseen.

It arrives without warning,
A flash of electric blue, blinding.
A wave of heat surges, swelling,
Its breath— a furnace, searing, unyielding.

It wraps its arms around me,
Smoke and flame entwined.
A smoldering embrace that lingers,
Unsatisfied, eternally hungry.

All-consuming, all-engulfing,
Burning deeper into my soul.
This is agony—
Rising once again within me.

Reach

I sense you there, just a breath below,
Your warmth flickering, faint but aglow.
My hands dig deep, though the earth resists,
Driven by love that forever persists.

Warrior

You carried a warrior's fire,
An unbreakable strength.
No path too daunting, no dream too vast,
Every challenge met, every moment grasped.

We were twin souls, two parts of one whole,
Bound by a love that time could not control.
In the end, we parted, your light dimmed,
But you remain, forever etched within.

Your demise revealed a shadowed place,
A land laced with poison and bait.
The ground bends like a crescent moon,
Its frown deepens, forever doomed.

I never cared for that place,
And now I care even less.
Ignorance hides behind its walls,
Its tall grass concealing its mess.

The blackest day was when we brought you home,
Curtains drawn, silence thick as stone.
We laid you down, wrapped like Snow White,
Time stood still, caught in endless night.

You are the pulse within my veins,
The fire that transcends this plane.
Your spirit now roams in fields of peace,

A place where shadows and darkness cease.

It rained the day we buried you,
Hiding the tears that fell like dew.
We wrapped you gently, a newborn at rest,
And laid you where the meadow is blessed.

Now you soar, free of mortal chains,
Through golden fields, where no shadow remains.
Your flame burns bright, eternal, and true,
For in my heart, I carry you.

Virus

Hate is like the flu—
If you're not careful, it will catch you,
Spreading like wildfire among the weak,
Thriving where kindness dares not speak.

It lingers, ravenous and blind,
Feeding on fear, unkind.
Some shake it off, their hearts immune,
While others fall beneath its tune.

Hate infects, it seeps within,
A force that twists and darkens skin.
But love— a flame, steady and slow—
Burns through the dark, refusing to go.

Salty Lips

Hot tears, unbidden—
Welling at the edges of tired eyes.
Falling heavy, slow,
Salt searing along trembling lips.

A bitter sting lingers—
Not sharp, but endless.
Each tear, a fragment breaking free,
A piece of me dissolving into the sea.

Grief presses close—
An unyielding pulse.
A weight folding deep into my chest,
Pressing, pressing—still pressing.

Memories return—
Clawing, tearing, relentless.
A tide swelling, thick and black,
Dragging me under its crushing ache.

My heart aches with its burden,
Heavy, raw, infinite.
While my mind drifts further inward,
Curling tight, silent, alone.

Butterflies

Vivid butterflies swarm my throat,
Wings trembling, restless.
They flutter down into my chest,
A storm of ache beneath my ribs.

The fury fades—
Feathered flurries slacken,
Yet they spiral deeper still,
Curling tight within the pit of me.

A fragile hope stirs—
Faint, uncertain.
Like the hush after weeping,
Too delicate to trust, but there.

They rage again—
Twisting my insides, relentless.
Pressing hard against breath and bone,
A fury I cannot quiet.

I crave escape—
To feel nothing and forget everything.Anything
to silence the ache-
 Of what's left behind.

Silent Storms

What they see—
A painted shore, calm and pale.
Lips curved where silence lingers,
The sea, glass-flat, betrays nothing.

But beneath—
Winds coil low, pressing inward.
A hush so sharp it cuts,
The tide rising, swelling behind my ribs.

Waves break in shadows,
A violence no eye can trace.
Frost clings, whisper-thin,
Its chill sinking deeper than skin.

The storm churns—
Feral, relentless, unnamed.
A ruin stitched beneath my veins,
The eye turning, turning, turning.

And though the world will never know,
Beneath the hush,
behind the glow—
The silent hurricane still grows.

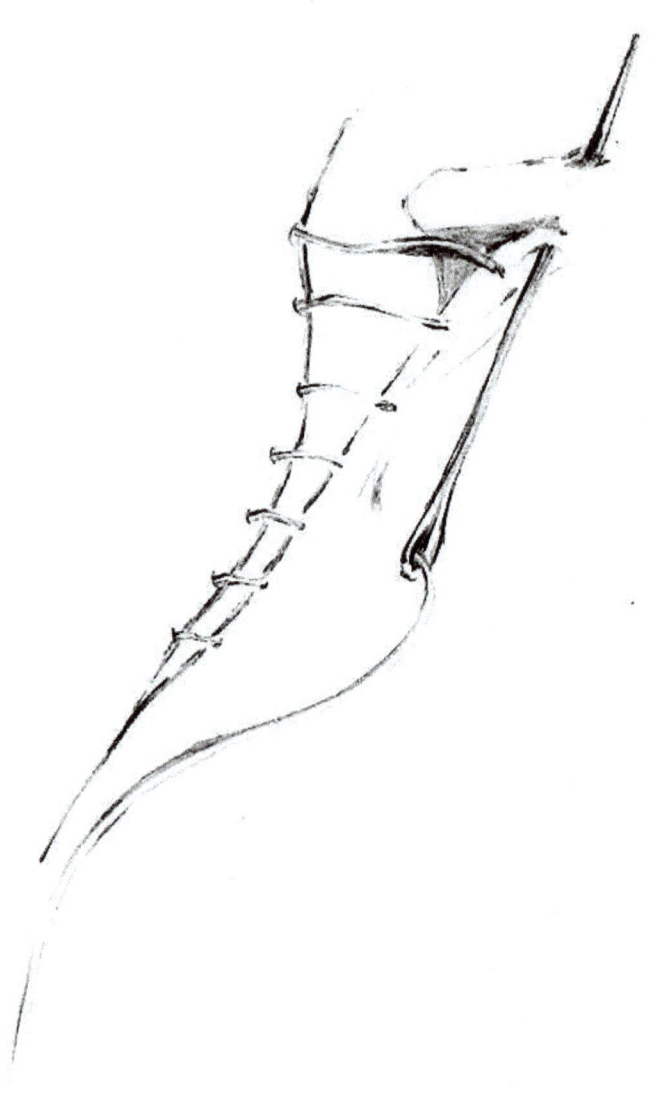

38

Stitch

In shadows deep, where memories reside,
They dance and haunt, a ceaseless tide.
Today, I grasp a scalpel's cold embrace,
And slice through to my heart's own space.

Poison spills, pooling on the floor,
Peeling the layers, row by row.
My hands delve in, the ache explored,
Uncovering wounds that quietly grow.

Stitch by stitch, I mend my core,
Yet still it lingers— the ache, the stain.
Threads weave through marrow and vein,
Binding the pain I can't ignore.

In Plath's realm, I confront my fear,
The weight of shadows still lingering near.
But through the stitches, light breaks in,
And hope starts where healing begins.

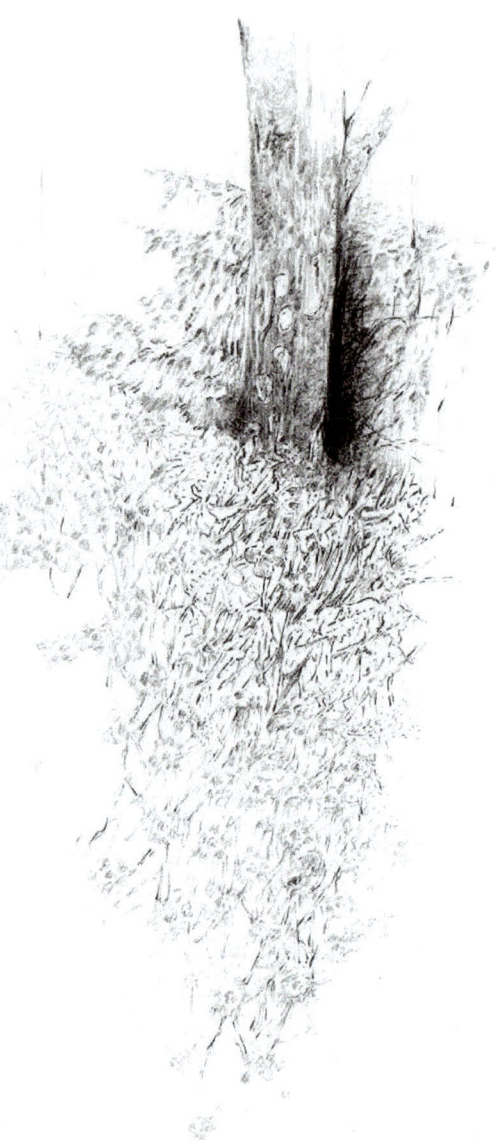

Whistle In The Wind

Are you where the wind whistles through the
trees,
Or in the waves that dance upon the seas?
Are you the warmth in the sun's embrace,
Or the cool shadow in a quiet place?

Do you linger in the bloom of spring,
In the songs that birds softly sing?
Are you the echo that fades too soon,
Or the silver glow beneath the moon?

River

Footfalls echo along a hidden trail,
Leading me to a place where secrets sail.
Quiet fills the air as I wander alone,
Drawn to whispers carved into stone.

I come upon a river's bend,
Where the path curves along a mountain's edge,
Purple and pink lupins idly by,
Watching and marking time with ripples that flow
on by.

The river whispers truths untold,
Its surface shimmering with souls of old.
Leaning closer, I see them now—
Reflections of those who shaped this world
somehow.

Some are souls who left too soon,
They loved life and feared no ghouls.
Others linger, their hearts still beating,
Bound to the earth, fleeting and meeting.

The most mysterious come last—
Unborn souls, their time not yet cast.
They will live beyond my final breath,
Guiding an age unknown to death.

Each ripple carries a reminder clear—

We drift through life, together, near.
Aligned in rows, each one flows,
A testament to all that eternity knows.

Flower Cuttings

Purple, pink, red,
Orange, yellow, white—
A palette of hues, destined to fade,
Each bloom sold at a price.

When they're ready and ripe,
It's time to say goodbye.
To roots, to earth,
To the family they left behind.

Their brilliance is clipped, confined to a vase,
Petals glowing under the sun's embrace.
But soon, the water grows still and dry,
And one by one, the petals lie.

Whispers of endings linger near,
A quiet elegy soft and clear.
Their beauty wilts, their stems lie bare,
Ghosts of grace now linger there.

Happiness and Madness

They come like thieves in the night,
Stealing moments with shadowed delight.
Fleeting and fragile, they quickly fade,
Yet in my memory, their embers are laid.

Happiness and madness cling as one,
Dancing together beneath the sun.
Bound by a delicate, invisible string,
Each a spark of life, a fleeting sting.

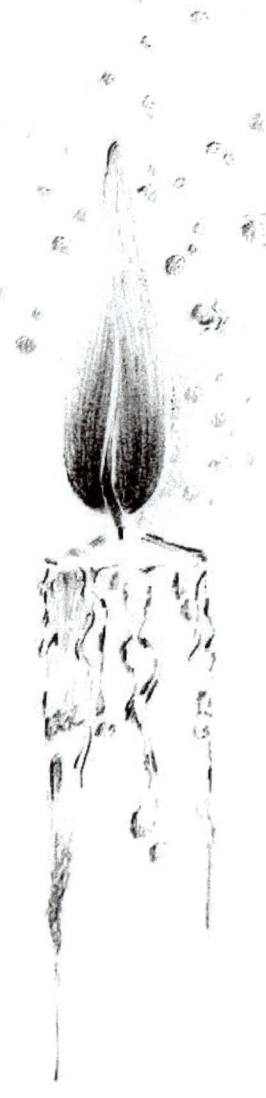

Power Cut

In a moment, our reliance is revealed,
Self-sufficiency— repealed by evolution.
A leash around our necks, we tread,
Toward another's spark, we're led.

In the hush of a power cut, I retreat,
Shadowed in the night's humid heat.
A single candle flickers by my side,
Its glow steady, my thoughts untied.

Birds murmur their soft goodnights,
Cicadas hum their morning rites.
My mind drifts, freed from screens and sound,
Roaming where silence and peace abound.

Outside, the world transforms anew,
Each rustle, each chirp, sharp and true.
I gaze into the candle's flame,
Shadows dance, playing their gentle game.

How strange the hush when the hum is gone,
Without our lifeline, we feel undone.
Yet in this quiet, a truth remains—
We crave the stillness we rarely sustain.

Be Mine

I saw love and asked it if it could be mine.
"I will be," it whispered, soft and divine.
I breathed, and the sun filled my chest,
Warming my heart, my soul, and all the rest.

Now it stands on the other side of the door,
A quiet echo, nothing more.
I feel my soul burn where my heart should be,
Its beat stolen, it's sound is lost to me.

Valley Of Unspoken

Words

I rehearsed my lines, my words prepared,
But when the moment came, my courage
disappeared.
My voice betrayed me, my heart stood still,
And every practiced word slipped down the hill.

Now they linger, a shadowed refrain,
A silent echo, a tender pain.
In this valley where words remain unsaid,
They haunt the space where courage fled.

The Ice Cream Truck

It's so hot, I fear I might just faint,
Dizzy with the mirages my mind paints.
The melody of the ice cream truck drifts on
near,
Yet, there's no one, no sound, nothing clear.

Out on this deserted, scorching road,
The asphalt burns a fiery load.
Perhaps I should warn the ice cream man-
His tires will surely melt where it stands.

Then again, I might let it get stuck,
A treasure trove of treats- just my luck!

Longing

Clenched teeth, a tearing chest,
Waves of pain, sadness unhinged.
A deep longing, an ache that remains,
An absence that echoes, a void that pains.
I miss all of it—
The moments, the touch,
Now, I sit in silence, crushed.

60

Waiting Room

White walls close in,
Stealing my breath.
My name pinned to a list—
No turning back, no escape from this.

I sit beneath the fluorescent hum,
Caught in its silent, radioactive drum.
Sterile fumes creep into my lungs,
Every corner echoes the scent of death.

I hold my breath, but it makes no difference,
My eyes are closed, yet I'm still imprisoned.
The waiting room swallows the minutes whole,
Its silence gnawing at my soul.

Where the Wild Things

Play

Buzzy bees buzz and play,
Chickens race on trikes al day.
Mischievous monkeys climb and sing,
Lions roar like kings of everything.

Shy deer peek and watch the fun,
Butterflies pirouette in the sun.
Swans playhouse on the lake so near,
Unrestrained, it's wild out here!

64

Etched

I memorized your touch—
The gentle weight of your hand atop mine.
The strong thumps of your heart, steady and
true,
As I pressed my ear to your chest, listening to
you.

A lullaby I still carry,
Even though you're gone.
I remember you,
And the thrill of you being alive.

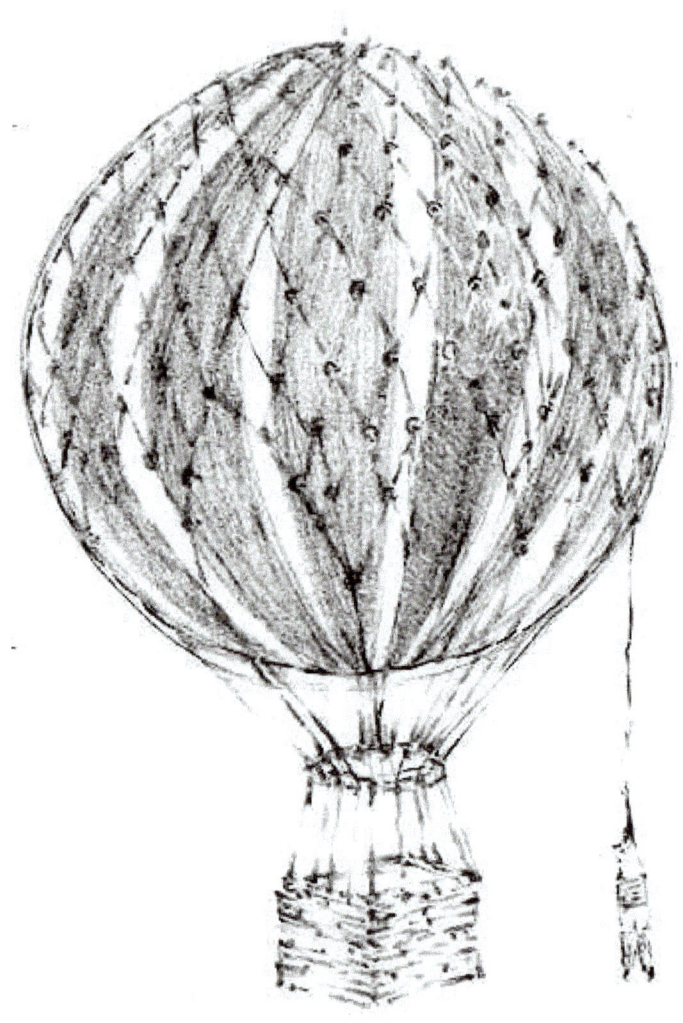

A Room Full of Dreams

Bright sunlight bounces off the green landscape,
Through an unseen window,
And into your room full of dreams.

Inanimate objects spring to life,
Planes soar, blue, red, and white,
Dipping and zooming with great delight.

A hot air balloon,
Candy cane red and white striped,
Idly floats below the ceiling, held by an
invisible string.

Meanwhile, a rainbow of dinosaurs parade below,
Stomping up and down the walls,
Looking for food, for treats to loot.

In the midst of all this magic, you lie on the
floor,
Mind far away,
Foot on the pedal.

Around the speedway you go, go, go,
Turning left, driving at the speed of light,
The only winner in sight!

In a world of wonder, pure and bright,
There is innocence, endless possibilities,
A treasure I hope you'll always keep!

Sweetness

The distant rush of cars hums outside,
Contrasting the quiet in here where you reside.
Your steady breathing, a true lullaby,
Time slows as your tiny chest lifts and sighs.

Delicate as a dandelion, full of dreams,
I watch over you, bathed in moonbeams.
Your rosy cheeks and gentle grace,
Tiny hands resting in their perfect place.

Each breath a metronome of hope,
A quiet drum that whispers for me to cope.
There's still room in this world, I know,
For love and peace to softly grow.

Acknowledgements

I am deeply thankful to the team at Author Book Publication for their support in transporting the manuscript into this book and bringing it into the world.

To my readers thank you for drifting between worlds with me. I hope these words resonate with you as much as they do with me.

I extend my love and gratitude to Shaz van Brandenburg for the stunning illustrations that brought this book to life.

I am also thankful to Val Leveson for nudging me to write. Thank you to Rebecca Wesseling for your strength and support during the difficult time following Lana's passing.

Finally, I would like to express my love and gratitude to my husband, Sam Angus, my greatest guru and anchor to every storm.

And to Lana, as a child, you were the dream I held closest to my heart. When I grew up, I found you, and you were so much more than I ever imagined. Though you've moved on, your song continues in every word I write. This book is, and always will be, for you.
Love,
Paris Delaney